The Least Beastly Among Us

By: Bernard "Burn" Loeffke

One hundred percent of the royalties from the sale of this book goes to

White House Fellows Foundation and Association
1750 Pennsylvania Ave. NW, Suite 300
Washington, DC 20006

www.helpingotherstoday.com

Published by **The Silver Scribers**, at John Knox Village in Pompano Beach, Florida, whose mission is to encourage senior authors to write their memoirs as a lasting legacy for their children and grandchildren.

Acknowledgements

This special edition honors John Gardner who created the White House Fellows. It is this program that has helped so many of us to live meaningful lives.

There is much to be thankful for.

Food For The Poor, a South Florida charitable organization, has made the dream of this soldier come true. We have created a circle of Communities of Hope in the Western Hemisphere for the Poor. The dream is to showcase an area where U.S. and Chinese citizens can work together to help the poor.

This special edition remembers two soldiers, one from China and the other from the U.S. who exemplify what it means to care for others (see pages 6 and 7).

Two of my White House Fellows classmates come to mind. Charles Gentry, a wounded soldier, and Tom O'Brien who is one of the most selfless individuals I know.

Former Captain "Ike" Leggett of the 199th LIB, the 2019 recipient of the Legacy Award for his actions to the communities he served.

David Sanchez, who financially has made possible for West Point cadets to get to China to teach preventative medicine in elementary schools.

Dr. Carmen Queral who has worked countless hours helping to write and prepare our books for the publisher.

Finally, Marty Lee who volunteers countless hours helping seniors write their memoirs. He has given many a vision that helps keep them motivated.

"I am not afraid of others not understanding me.
I am afraid of not understanding others."
– Confucius

About the Author

Burn Loeffke is a West Point Graduate. He has a B.S. in Engineering, an M.A. in Russian, and a Ph.D. in Political Science. He has taught Graduate School at Georgetown University.

He has commanded parachute units, Special Forces, and combat infantry units. He culminated his military career as the Commanding General of Army South. In his military service, he accumulated more than 250 parachute jumps – two in combat in Vietnam.

Loeffke has been awarded the Purple Heart for wounds in combat, as well as several Valor Awards. A Ranger and pilot, he is the first foreigner to have jumped with Chinese Army Units – a distinction he earned when assigned as the Chief of Military Mission to China. He was an Army Attaché in Moscow. He has served as a Staff Officer in the White House and was the Director of the Commission on White House Fellows.

An important ingredient in General Loeffke's life is physical fitness. He has been an advisor to the President's Council on Physical Fitness and has won swimming championships while in the Army. He also competed in a military decathlon in Russia and ran full-length marathons in China.

After retirement in 1992, he went to medical school to become a medical officer. He now serves on medical missions abroad.

For other books written by the author, Burn Loeffke, visit the website: www.helpingotherstoday.com

Forward

Burn Loeffke is an American hero who has lived life to the fullest. He has served his nation in war, peacemaking and in reconciliation. He is both a warrior and a diplomat. In the latest chapter of his remarkable life, he has dedicated himself to the healing arts and to passing on what he has learned to his children and to all our children.

Burn has been a friend of mine for 25 years. He has a generous spirit and it is as natural as breathing for him to dedicate this book and its proceeds to the memory of a fallen hero, Sgt. Larry Morford.

So read, enjoy and be inspired by these stories and have your faith restored.

Colin L. Powell General,
USA (Retired)

China 1973

White House Fellows Burn Loeffke (left) and Colin Powell (right).

In Memoriam: Two Soldiers

Sergeant Larry Morford
U.S. Army (199th LIB)
Died at age 22 serving his country

The biographer Blankfort writes, "few are won by principles alone but by those who preach and live them.

It was the example of Christ not his sermons that conquered his followers.

Sgt. Morford was a soldier in the unit I commaded in Vietnam. Larry did not believe in war as the way to resolve conflicts. I once asked him why if he felt this way, had he volunteered for Vietnam and combat duty. He reponded, "Sir, the job you and I are doing is the job of a beast and the least beastly of us should be doing it." That was Larry's sermon and he backed it up by voluntering for dangerous missions.

Sgt. Morford was killed leading a patrol a few days before he was to return home.

It is because of Sgt. Morford that I became a medical officer.

In Memoriam: Two Soldiers

Corporal Lei Feng
People's Liberation Army
Died at age 22 serving his country

Lei Feng became an orphan after his mother and father died at age 6. The state sent him to an orphanage and at age 16, he joined the army.

He was always helping those in need without thinking of himself. "It is the people and the government who have given me a second life. I will put my limited life into the unlimited service to the people."

Lei Feng was killed in an accident. In his honor the army published his diary. The nation was moved by his life story and his service to those in need. He inspired many, especially the young. In 1963, Mao Zedong called on the nation to "Learn from Lei Feng." When the first team of US Global Volunteers arrived in China in 1996, the media called them the "American Lei Fengs." One newspaper wrote, "Lei Feng has returned from the US."

Lei Feng has become part of the Chinese language. It is a synonym for volunteering dedication and selfless service.

Trust

To my right a Chinese General. In 1982, there was no insignia of rank. The only insignia that everyone wore was a red star on the cap.

It was China in the early 1980s. For months I had been trying to parachute jump with Chinese paratroopers. The answer was always the same, "No."

I was told, "You are the first U.S. Army General to be assigned to China. We cannot afford to have you injured." My luck changed when U.S. Secretary of Defense, Caspar "Cap" Weinberger visited China and asked that I be allowed to jump. When the Chinese responded that I might be injured, Mr. Weinberger replied, "I have hundreds of Generals in the Pentagon. If he dies, I will send you another one." Everyone laughed. Within two weeks, I was training in preparation to become the first American to jump with the Chinese army.

Trust builds strong relationships. The request to jump was approved, but the Chinese wanted me to jump with my own U.S. parachute packed by U.S. riggers.

My answer: "I want to use a Chinese parachute packed by Chinese riggers." They agreed to my request after an hour of negotiations. They asked that at a minimum, I be present at the packing of the chute and that I keep the parachute with me until the day of the jump. I replied that I did not need to be present for the packing and that the parachute should stay with the other chutes. I wanted them to know that I was trusting them with my life.

The jump and the time I spent with the paratroopers created a bond that would be difficult in the absence of danger.

Mutual respect and trust are important ingredients in any relationship.

Introduction

NO SHAKING HANDS POLICY
1954-1972
"You are forbidden to have contact with the Chinese. If you come face to face with the Chinese take a cold attitude towards them."
Guidance given by then Secretary of State
~ J. F. Dulles (1954)

In traditional Chinese ideograms, the concept of friendship comes from the shaking of hands. The ideogram YO (friend) was initially two hands moving in the same direction, two hands cooperating for a common purpose. It later evolved into two hands clasping each other in friendship.

In ancient times, the word 'peace' meant "to bind together." The concept was to bind friends so closely together that peace was the end result. In China, to be called a 'LAO PENGYOU' (old friend) takes time. But once you have become one, the relationship is cemented.

For more than 18 years, U.S. and Chinese diplomats did not shake hands. In 1972. President Nixon visited China and shook hands with Chinese officials starting a new era of U.S./Sino relations.

The shaking of hands is a start, but the real test is trust.

An American who is admired and trusted is Colin Powell. His trip to China in 1973 with White House Fellows helped him to understand the Middle Kingdom.

Indian Chief and author in Brazilian Amazon Jungle. 1966

What follows is an alphabet of letters that touch
on some aspect of leadership.

Table of Contents

美

America

The word *America* came from a European discoverer named Americus Vespucius, who landed in what is today South America. The name became so popular that those who lived in the northern part of our hemisphere adopted it. In this hemisphere we are all Americans, North, Central and South Americans.

America also means *Beautiful*. The Chinese have chosen (out of more than 60,000 ideograms) the ideogram *Mei*, which is the word beautiful for America. We are called people of the beautiful country.

The ideogram Mei is the combination of two other ideograms: sheep and big. A sheep in Chinese is considered a mild-mannered animal with a gentle disposition. The ideogram for big translates as large, powerful and

significant. The ideogram for sheep, initially, was a simple drawing showing the upside-down horns and a tail. It later evolved into six strokes depicting the horns, the ears, the lets and the tail. Big depicts a man with is arms stretched out.

The combination of Sheep + Big means a mature person who has a mild and gentle disposition and who is admirable and beautiful.

羊 + 大 = 美

There are many factors that serve to unite us. Millions of Chinese have come to the U.S., became citizens and have children born here. They form a bridge between us. An example is the 14-year old, Peter Wang, who was killed in 2018 in his high school in Florida while saving his classmates from a gunman.

There is much we can do together. The environment, rising seas, near earth objects (NEOs) that threaten to destroy our fragile planet. We are cooperating in the field of Stem Cell Research to help cure disease. Let's concentrate on cooperating instead of confronting. Let's begin. God Bless America.

US and Vietnamese paratroopers. Vietnam, 1964

Buddies

What is more precious than life? In World War II, when a US Army group was ambushed, a seriously wounded soldier laid under the enemy's fire, unable to move. The officer in charge determined the risk was too great for rescue, but the wounded man's friend disregarded the orders and ran to rescue his friend. When he returned, carrying his friend who had died, he too had been mortally wounded. The Officer, crying with anger, yelled, "I told you not to go. Now I have lost two good men. It wasn't worth it."

The dying soldier looked up and gasped, "Sir, it was worth it, because when I got to him, he whispered, "Jim, I knew you'd come."

> ***"Pity the man who falls and has no one to help him up."***
> —*Ecclesiastes 4:10*

"I will prepare myself and my chance will come."
— *Abraham Lincoln*

Checklist

Benjamin Franklin, in his quest for improvement, found it useful to evaluate his progress daily by means of a checklist. Every evening he would check off those attributes he felt needed improvement. He recounted that the quality of humility was a weak point of his. Whenever a week went by that he had no check marks by the trait of humility, he felt proud of being so humble and had to check the humility block again.

Here is our family's version of Mr. Franklin's checklist:

	M	T	W	Th	F	S	S
1. Humility							
2. Charity (Did I give to someone or something unselfishly?)							
3. Cleanliness (Was I neat and orderly?)							
4. Silence (Did I engage in trivial conversation? Did I listen?)							
5. Perseverance (Did I keep my goals?)							
6. Fairness (Did I treat others fairly?)							
7. Frugality (Did I purchase unnecessary things?)							
8. Moderation (Did I over-eat or over-drink?)							
9. Sincerity (Was I sincere in words and action?)							
10. Tranquility (Was I disturbed by trifles?)							
11. Thoughtfulness (Did I think of someone else's feelings ahead of mine?)							
12. Cheerfulness (Did I make someone feel good by smiling?)							

Détente

I used to explain détente to soldiers with this illustration: Picture two archers who are facing each other with bows that are taut. As they face each other, one takes a suspicious step and one archer lets go of his arrow. The other one does the same. Both arrows strike the target and both archers are killed. Under détente, the tension on the bows of both of these archers would be released slowly until little tension remained on the bows. If a misunderstanding occurred, there would be plenty of time for dialogue as both sides were putting more tension on their bows.

Détente is a relaxation of tension. This is good for the world. It is the mission of all leaders to help keep hope alive by relaxing tensions with their neighbors. Respectful dialogue brings a relaxation of tensions.

> *"No medicine is powerful enough*
> *to overcome a lust for vengeance."*
> — *Chinese*

"Our citizenship is in Heaven."
— *Philippians 3:20*

Enemy

My son used to ask, "Dad, why do soldiers have to fight? You were a soldier; did you hate your enemy?"

How do you explain to your five-year old that you spent four years fighting people you did not know and did not hate? The answer that came to mind was, we need to work hard to avoid having enemies.

Senator John Glenn was our first astronaut. He recounts that in his space voyage, he had been given a series of cards in foreign languages to be used in case of an emergency. He noticed that in many languages the words stranger and enemy were the same. One incredible American, Stan Cottrell, has a unique way of making friends out of strangers. Stan, who ran forty miles a day for forty days, made a difference in Sino-U.S. relations in his great friendship run from the Great Wall of China to the tip of Southern China. The fifty-year-old American met more Chinese during his run than any of us had in our years in China. Stan then invited three Chinese champions to run from San Francisco to Washington, where President Bush greeted them. Personal relations build strategies. In China, as in everywhere else, relationships are important. Friendship is valued. We need to make sure we make friends out of strangers.

DEAR COLONEL,
I THANK YOU...

Foxhole

The war in Vietnam was hard on our soldiers. We were always looking for ways to increase morale. The Foxhole Exchange Program was something the troops accepted with enthusiasm. A Captain would identify the best soldier in his unit, and I would send him back to sleep in my tent, while I replaced him in his unit. This allowed me to observe and feel what our soldiers were experiencing. The exchange program was a great morale booster, as all the soldiers wanted to sleep in my tent and eat hot meals in the rear. It didn't work miracles, but it was appreciated. I remember one letter in particular:

Dear Colonel,

I thank you for letting me exchange places with you. The men also appreciate what you are doing. However, I still don't like the Army, and I still don't like officers. As a matter of fact, my favorite prayer goes this way: "O Lord, distribute bullets as you do the pay; let the officers get most of them."

Respectfully,

Citizen Jenkins

> *"Everything I did in my life that was worthwhile,*
> *I caught hell for."*
> — *Chief Justice Earl Warren*

Geese

I remember my first tour in Vietnam. The Air Force would drop, by parachute, boxes full of live chickens and ducks. Vietnamese troops would place these animals out on the perimeter as guards. They were excellent security. Ducks, especially, would alert at the slightest movement in their vicinity. As our food supply dwindled, we would eat the ducks and chickens. The Vietnamese soldier would march with a live chicken or duck inside his backpack. It made for an interesting sight, to see duck heads sticking out of a long row of packs.

History tells us that the Romans also used geese to warn them of intruders. We have forgotten many useful history lessons and spent billions on technology when in some instances, security and nourishment can be provided with just a few quackers.

"Wisdom is better than weapons of war."
— Ecclesiastes 9:18

*"If more grownups would do more good,
our generation would have fewer wrongs to fix."*
— An eighth grade student

Heaven

When Marc, our son, was five years old, he once asked, "Daddy, do all poor people go to heaven?" I answered, "What do you think?" Marc responded, "Poor people go to heaven because they have been poor, and anyway, Dad, how can poor people be bad – if they don't have any money?" Before answering I asked, "How about rich people? Do they go to heaven?" His answer: "Rich people could go to heaven if they don't complain about their money and do something good with their money."

The dialogue continued. "Son, are we rich?" "No, Dad, we are not rich. We are in the middle – between rich and poor." "Do we go to heaven?" I asked. The answer: "I think we go to somewhere in the middle, between heaven and hell."

I thought that this was the appropriate time to say, "Son, it is not a sin to be rich. What matters is what we do with the money we have. Jesus taught that from those who have much, much is expected."

I then added that the concept of doing good is also good for the one who does it. It has been shown that we strengthen our immune systems when we do acts of love, such as helping our neighbor. I ended our conversation by telling him about one our most admired soldiers. General Vessey used to say, "The relationship between man and man is bad because the relationship between man and God is bad." He would then add, "It is hard to be a good soldier in the Army of the Lord, as many find it difficult to live by the rule of 'Do unto others as you would have them do unto you.'"

"Whoever wants to be first among you must be a slave to all."
– Mark 10:44

Interpreter

When I was a young lieutenant, I was asked to report to General Stilwell. This general had the reputation of eating young officers for breakfast. He was, at the time, the Chief of Staff of our Parachute Corps, a position I would assume some twenty years later. He asked that I translate his remarks to officers of the Brazilian War College. My efforts to interpret his remarks were Herculean but fell short of what was required. I had not looked at a Portuguese book or spoken the language since I had left West Point.

General Stilwell also spoke for a long time, making it difficult to remember everything he said, and I know I left out several points. The general ended his presentation with an anecdote. I informed the Brazilian officers that I did not know how to translate the joke and respectfully requested that they please laugh at the general's joke. The Brazilians roared and General Stilwell was satisfied with the talk and my promotion to captain was assured.

From this experience, I learned the importance of interpreters, as they can change what is said. Someone needs to check the interpreter. Better yet, learn the language. Languages are the doors to friendship.

> *"Medicine cures everyone not fated to die."*
> — *Chinese*

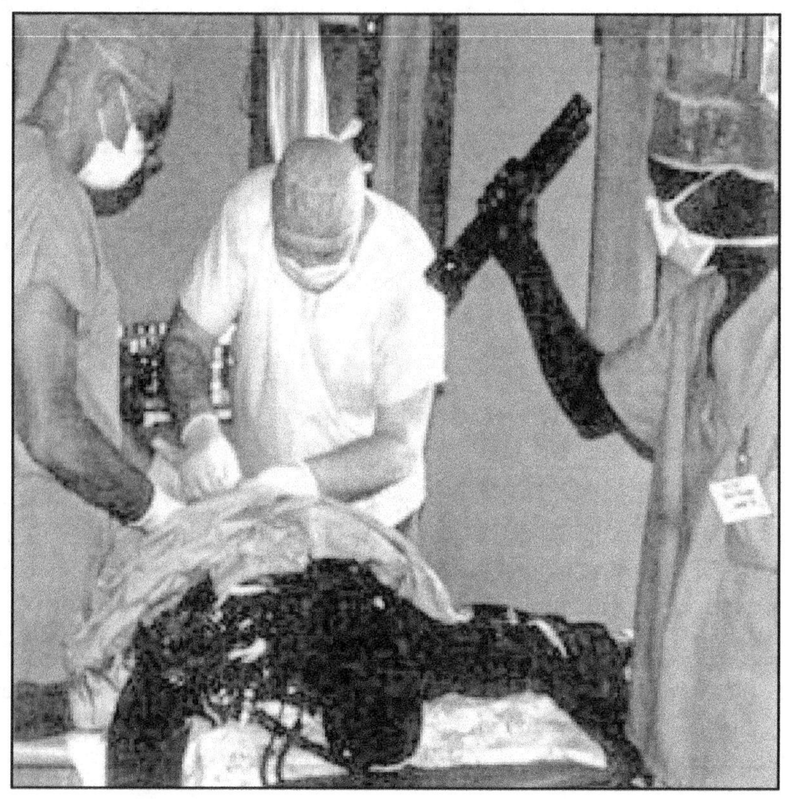

Author on the left Sudan, 1997. Surgery by flashlight and running water provided by Africans with buckets from the river.

Jefferson

Our second president captured the essence of good government when he said, "God grant that men of principles shall be our principal men."

Other great men from other lands have made similar statements. Simon Bolivar remarked, "The way to make yourself popular and to govern well is to employ honest men even though they might be adversaries."

In 2003, I served in countries where adversaries chose not to forgive or forget. Iraq, Kosovo, and Northern Ireland had clusters of people who lived for revenge.

It was in Northern Ireland, however, where our family has spent three summers. Our son Marc, who was fourteen at the time, helped raise $10,000 dollars to send Protestant and Catholic children to a reconciliation camp. It is in Northern Ireland where walls exist as high as those built to separate East from West Berlin. The government calls them peace walls that have been erected to separate Protestants from Catholics. The people call them hate walls. Our family is committed to Northern Ireland as we are convinced that we will not be able to deliver a message of peace as long as Christians continue to treat each other as enemies.

"Do not be overcome by evil but overcome evil with good."
— Romans 12:2

GOOD!
WHAT IS..
LSC

Kissinger

Dr. Kissinger was considered a genius in foreign policy and an outstanding teacher. Many of us had a chance to gain insights of these two characteristics while we worked for him in the White House.

He emphasized that success in government, as well as in any endeavor, depended on assistants who were loyal, possessed great stamina, and were competent. Loyalty was essential for harmony between leader and follower. Without loyalty, no organization could survive.

Stamina was needed to work long hours, day in and day out. Of what good is genius if it tires easily. Stamina is needed for hard jobs that require much energy and exposure to stress.

Competence, he would add, was not difficult to find; but the combination of loyalty, stamina, and competence was not found in many.

"People may see and admire your talent,
but they will remember and cherish your love."
— *Huffy*

*"Do everything possible on your part to
live in peace with everybody."*
— *Romans 12:18*

Liberty

One of my frequent satisfactions when I served in Washington, DC was visiting the Organization of American States and being greeted by the Latin American guard with, "Buenos dias, General de hombres libres (Good morning, General of free men)." The greeting made me reflect on the lives that have been lost defending that freedom. Those who have lost their freedom explain, "Freedom is being unafraid of your government. Freedom is walking tall. Freedom is being able to pursue happiness as long as it does not violate the freedom of others."

Freedom needs to be protected and nurtured. Volunteers are needed everywhere to assist those less fortunate in our communities.

"Train up a child in the way he should go,
and when he is old he will not depart from it."
— *Proverbs 22:6*

First American to jump in communist China, 1984.

Midwife

Language and the differences in cultures continue to create misunderstandings. When I served in China, a Chinese general read my biography and was surprised at one of my specialties. The general had noticed that I was a midwife, which translates in Chinese as "half a wife." The general commented that in China you can only be a full wife or no wife at all, but it is very difficult to be half a wife. Could I explain? That was the first of many questions that I tried to answer during my years in the Middle Kingdom. Good relationships protect us from misunderstood words.

"Make no promises when you are seized with joy;
write no letters when you are seized with anger."
— *Chinese*

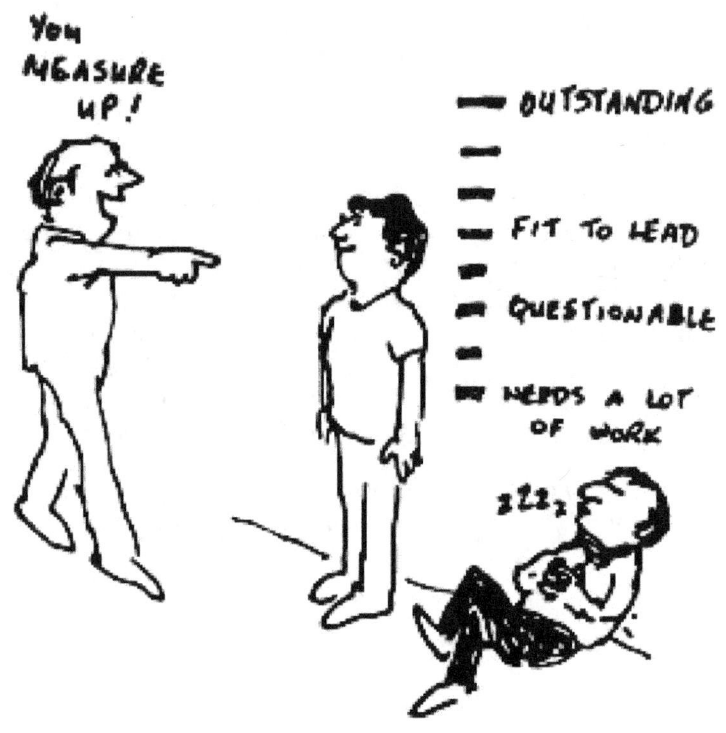

"What does the Lord require of you? Justice, love, kindness and to walk humbly with your God."
— *Micah 6:8*

Norms

The military is known for its "norms" that have to be followed. My years teaching civilians have convinced me that many of the "norms" that are needed for successful leadership in the military are also needed for civilian life. These are dedication, hard work, and sacrifice. Good leaders are ethical, dedicated and willing to sacrifice for a good cause.

A former President of Argentina, Carlos Pellegrini, explained the "norms" of the military within a nation as follows:

"The military man has other duties and other rights than a civilian; he obeys other laws; has other judges; dresses differently; he even speaks and walks in a different manner. The military man has the privilege to be armed among citizens that are unarmed. We entrust our flag to him. We give him the keys to our fortresses and our arsenals. We entrust our conscripts and the authority to dispose of their freedom, their will, and even their lives.

"With one signal of his sword, our battalions move, our fortresses open, the national flag is raised or lowered, and all this privilege we give him under one sole and unique guarantee: the guarantee of his honor and his word. This is the yardstick by which our young leaders must be measured, to see if they have the necessary moral stature to wield the sword, which is the most glorious legacy of those heroes that gave us our country – to wear that uniform filled with gold and stripes that would be ridiculous tinsel, were it not for a tradition of dedication and sacrifices that bind those wearing it, as if they belonged to the clergy.

"Good leaders, no matter their profession, are willing to make sacrifices."

I'M DIALOGUED OUT!

Organizations

A Latin American general complimented the role of international organizations when he commented:

"Men hate each other, because they fear each other. They fear each other, because they don't understand each other. They don't understand each other, because they don't meet. Thank God for international organizations that provide the opportunity to meet and dialogue our differences."

Dialogue, and more dialogue, is needed to understand each other better.

If we keep talking to each other, we may eventually find something on which we can agree.

> *"There is nothing so annoying as to have two people*
> *go right on talking when you are interrupting."*
> — *Mark Twain*

DIRTY!
DISGUSTING!
HONK!
FUFFH!

Perceptions

Many North Americans are poorly informed of other cultures, because we are interested mainly in what is happening to us here at home. Unfortunately, the majority of the world is non-American. We are different, and we have to understand those differences and learn to walk inside other shoes. I am reminded of my experience in Vietnam with handkerchiefs. We considered Vietnamese dirty, because they blew their noses without handkerchiefs. The Vietnamese in turn considered us dirty, because we blew our noses into handkerchiefs and then carried our dirty handkerchiefs in our pockets. They called us dirt carriers. Perceptions can lead to wrong conclusions. We need to know the culture of other nations and organizations, before we make snap judgments.

5 Pillars of Islam

1. There is no God but Allah and Mohammed is his prophet and Allah is merciful and compassionate.
2. Pray five times a day facing towards Mecca.
3. Give to the poor.
4. Fast for 30 days once a year.
5. Pilgrimage to Mecca.

WE HONOR BY
REMEMBERING..

Question

How can we honor those who are no longer with us? The answer is simple, "Remember them." This poem remembers two very special people. It was written by a young man, Sergeant Larry Morford, to a woman he was never given the chance to make his wife. He was killed two weeks after writing it:

> Could I drink of a fountain of youth,
> whose wine is eternal life?
> They would be but bitter drugs
> if forever I had to live without
> the taste of your lips on mine,
> and without you as my eternal wife.
> And were I to hold all powers
> and rule over the universe as a god,
> and could my vision encompass
> all secrets transparently through;
> could I live forever, toppling
> all of the towers,
> I know this, a god is not a god,
> Without his goddess.

— January 1970, Vietnam

*"Love the Lord your God with all your heart and with
all your soul and with all your mind and with all your strength."*
— *Mark 12:30*

Religion

The good soldier should be a role model for the citizens the soldier protects. An American religious leader, Cardinal O'Neal, talks about the relationship between a military and a religious career:

"If I had not been a priest, I most certainly would have had to be a soldier, because they are both called to do the identical things – that is, preservation of peace, establishment of justice when it has been lost, and the providing of security, with protection for the weak and the innocent."

We can all be good soldiers, whether we wear a uniform or not, because selfless service is a large component of Good Leadership in any profession.

"No Muslim could be a true believer unless he
desires for his brother no less than
that which he desires for himself."
— *The Koran*

San Martin

Who was this man? Those who know his accomplishments consider him the greatest general who ever lived in the Americas. I know of no other leader, who received so willingly, his subordinates' obedience. What makes this man so special?

General San Martin was courageous, charitable, patient, and above all, a great teacher. He wrote a code of conduct that became the "Bible" of the good officer.

By age seventeen, he had fought for three countries. By his late twenties, he had become the uncontested military genius of the Americas. He demonstrated this genius by leading his army over the impenetrable Andes to defeat the Spanish in Chile. He then planned and led an amphibious campaign and liberated Peru. His insistence to not allow frictions between brothers to escalate into armed conflicts made him a forefather of conflict resolution. He declined political power, so that people could decide freely their own future.

He donated his salary to his soldiers and charities. He believed in equality and practiced it with his soldiers, who were Indians, Mestizos, and Blacks.

He did not amass wealth and thus died a poor man in material goods. But in love for his country and in his Christian charity for the peoples of the Americas, he was a rich man indeed, and a leader who gave his people hope.

> ***"Be humble, gentle, patient with one another.***
> ***Make every effort to keep unity through the bond of peace."***
> — *Ephesians 4:2-3*

T
T
T

The Three Ts

In the early 1900s, there were less than twelve democracies in the world. Today there are more than one hundred. But young democracies are fragile and need much help to survive.

In Latin America, I was told that if a leader hopes to be elected, the promise of the Three Ts has to be made; Tortillas, Trabajo and Techo, in other words; food, work and a roof over our heads.

We ask our leaders to perform miracles. It has been said that the principal role of a leader is to keep hope alive.

The US, as the leader of the democratic world, has the responsibility to assist these fledgling democracies in keeping hope alive. History tells us that no two truly freely elected democracies have ever fought each other. Our commitment to peace is to foster the climate for democracy to grow. One way is to help in providing the Three Ts.

"Let us consider how to provoke one another to
love and good deeds."
— *Hebrews 10:24-25*

Chinese champions arriving in Ft. Bragg, NC, after running from San Francisco, with author.

Unity

In Argentina, an admiral who had worked in an international organization told me that Argentina could not have solely an Argentine strategy.

"The vision of the future cannot be a selfish one. The future, if there is to be one, has to be a product of cooperation. There cannot be an Argentine, a Brazilian, or a US strategy. It has to be a common strategy, one that supports the well-being of all the people of our region, or it will support none."

This type of thinking is nurtured in international organizations. Peace and stability may be achieved when we can say that united, we are more, united we are kinder, and united we think of others more often.

We all thirst for heroes. One of these heroes was Captain Nathan Hale, who made this statement before he was executed by firing squad during North America's Revolutionary War:

"I regret that I have but one life to lose for my country."

What we need today are international heroes, who will teach us to cooperate with each other, and in this way avoid fighting each other.

"Where your treasure is, there your heart will also be."
— *Matthew 6:21*

JUNGLE
ROAD
PROJECT #4

Vision

In the late 1980s, we were directed to build a fifteen-mile road through the jungles of Ecuador. The work was hard and the conditions primitive. One of my greatest challenges was to "instill a vision," that would put fire in the bellies of 1,500 soldiers working in torrential rains with mosquitoes that seemed determined to carry us away, and Indians that had killed foreigners a week before.

The vision we created was that we were there to build a democracy by helping the development of the country. The two D's served us well, as every soldier could remember those two words: Democracy and Development. However, it soon became clear that a vision has to be sold to each person.

After four weeks on the project, I visited an engineering company, and asked one of the dump truck drivers what was his mission. He responded, "Sir, I dump rocks. I then go get more rocks and dump those rocks." When I asked how were his spirits, he responded, "Very low, I hate it here. I cannot wait to go home." Three miles down the road, I asked the same question of another dump truck driver. His answer gave me hope that the vision had taken hold of at least one person. "Sir, I am here building democracy. There can be no democracy without development. I am helping to build a road that will connect two towns that will help development in this country." When I asked how was his morale, he answered; "Great, I am making history, but I have a request. Get us more mechanics, so we can keep more trucks working around the clock." The vision gave this man a purpose that made his tough work bearable.

"Without a vision, people perish."
— *Proverbs 29:18*

US Presidents Who Served in the Military

George Washington, Virginia................................General, Commander, Army
Thomas Jefferson, Virginia............................ Colonel, Virginia Militia
James Madison, Virginia.............................. Colonel, Virginia Militia
James Monroe, Virginia....................................Major, Continental Army
Andrew Jackson, Tennessee.................................Major General, Indian Wars
William H. Harrison, Ohio.....................................Major General, War of 1812
John Tyler, Virginia.................................. Captain, Virginia Militia, War of 1812
James K. Polk, Tennessee ....Major, Tennessee Militia
Zachary Taylor, Kentucky .... Major General, Mexican War
Millard Fillmore, New York .... Major, Home Guard
Franklin Pierce, NH .... Brigadier General, Militia, Mexican War
James Buchanan, PA.....................................Private, Militia, War of 1812
Abraham Lincoln, Illinois.............................. Captain, Militia, Black Hawk War
Andrew Johnson, Tennessee .... Brigadier General, Volunteers, Civil War
Ulysses S. Grant, Illinois...................................General, Mexican War, Civil War
Rutherford Hayes, Ohio ....Brevet Major General, Civil War
James A. Garfield, Ohio .... Major General, Volunteers, Civil War
Chester A. Arthur, New York .... Brigadier General, Militia, Civil War
Benjamin Harrison, Indiana........................ Brevet Brigadier General, Civil War
William McKinley, Ohio .... Brevet Major, Volunteers, Civil War
Theodore Roosevelt, New York .... Colonel, Spanish-American War
Harry S. Truman, Missouri .... Colonel, Reserve Corps, World War II
Dwight D. Eisenhower, New York....................General of the Army, World War II
John F. Kennedy, MA ....Lieutenant, Navy, World War II
Lyndon B. Johnson, Texas ....Commander, Navy, World War II
Richard M. Nixon, New York ....Commander, Navy, World War II
Gerald R. Ford, Michigan .... Lt. Commander, Reserve, World War II
James E. Carter, Georgia...Lieutenant, US Navy
Ronald W. Reagan, California...............Captain, Army Air Forces, World War II
George H. W. Bush, Texas....................................Lieutenant, Navy, World War II
George W. Bush, Texas.. Captain, Air Force

Washington

Washington was our first army commander and our first president. Washington was the first of a long list of presidents who experienced military life.

History shows that many of our leaders had military experience. Thirty-one out of forty-three U.S. presidents served in the military. Almost all of the first Latin American leaders were military men.

Military experience is one common bond that links a majority of presidents. Most US presidents served in the tradition of the citizen soldier, taking up arms to meet an emergency. For them, the concept of civilian supremacy over the military was a natural assumption, one reaffirmed by their presidential oath to support and defend the Constitution of the United States. The link between military service and presidential leadership directly reflects the founding fathers' vision of a military establishment accountable to the people.

Those of us in the military consider ourselves "Peacemakers." We have a strong interest in peace, for if negotiations fail, it is we who are called to suffer war's devastation. We will be the dead and the wounded.

"Integrity and firmness is all I can promise."
— George Washington on becoming the first President of the United States.

IS THIS THE WAY TO X?
LEFT
RIGHT

The Missing Ingredient

When we woke up today, one third of the world was experiencing some form of unrest; Neighbors fighting neighbors and distant wars that never seem to end.

The President of Czechoslovakia, when he visited Washington in 1990, gave a warning: "We still don't know how to put morality ahead of politics, science and economics. The salvation of this world lies nowhere else than in the human heart. Without a global revolution in the sphere of human consciousness, nothing will change for the better and the catastrophe towards which this world is headed, whether it be ecological, social, demographic or a general breakdown of civilization will be unavoidable."

"Whoever battles with monsters had better see that
it does not turn him into a monster."
— Friedrich Nietzsche

YANKEE GO HOME
YANKEE GO HOME
...AND WHEN YOU
GO HOME,
FLY
ARGENTINO
AIRLINE

Yankee

When I think of the letter "Y", I think of Yankee. When I think of Yankee, I think of "Yankee Go Home."

A placard I saw in Argentina was the first time I had seen the word Yankee used in a favorable light. The sign read, "Yankee Don't Go, but if you must, fly Argentinean Airlines."

The United States is still the place where the persecuted and afflicted want to come. Even those who hate us want to live in America. The US needs to continue to be generous and help those less fortunate. The Bible tells us that from those who have much, much is expected. We need to become a role model that others will want to emulate and not avoid.

Everywhere we turn volunteers are needed. Local and international communities cry out for help.

When our son was five, he would ask; "Dad, what can I do? I am just a child." My answer: "Son, you can help one less fortunate person at a time. You have many toys that you can give. You can also join us and visit people in nursing homes and hospitals." I reminded him that the Good Samaritan did not help a million people. He helped one.

Our daughter, Kristina, when she was 9, made animals out of balloons in the pediatric cancer wards in Central America. She was loved because she smiled, touched the children and selflessly stayed until every child had an animal. This is the sort of demonstration of love that will produce a "Yankee Don't Go" sign.

"But just as you excel in everything,
see that you also excel in this grace of giving."
— *2 Corinthians 8:7*

Sgt. Larry Morford (4/8/48 - 2/12/70)

*"Blessed are the peacemakers
for they shall be called the children of God."*
— *Matthew 5:9*

Z marks the end of our alphabet. This letter reminds me that our lives also have ends. When our stay on earth is concluded, what will they say about us? What will they write on our tombstones?

This collection of letters concludes with the thought that the future is not hopeless. My son used to remind me, "Dad, don't be sad; it's not too bad."

We witness daily despair, pain and evil. But good news also exists. The Mother Teresas exist. Journalists who brave threats and write the truth exist. Soldiers who believe and die defending human rights exist.

> **"The only thing that saves the world is the little handful of disinterested men in it. I have found a few. I wish I had found more. I can name two or three whom I have never found thinking about themselves or their own interests, and I tie myself to them as you would to an anchor. Men willing to die in obscurity, if only they might serve. The princes among us are those who forget themselves and serve mankind."**
>
> *— Former U.S. President Woodrow Wilson*

Will we be remembered as one of those princesses or princes?

Building Hope in Central America

Helping Others Today (H.OT.) builds relationships using educational tools to build healthy communities.

Central America is on the top of the list because of violence in the area.

Pictures of a home before (above), and a home after (below) financed by H.O.T. and Food For The Poor.

Our goal is to provide a roof, drinking water and a skill to bring the poor out of poverty.

To learn more on how you can help contact:
Food For The Poor 954-427-2222.

What Is the Future?

We can make it one of gloom or one of hope. The key is building trust.

The US and PRC wield immense economic, military, and political influence, yet each finds it difficult to engender mutual trust in the global arena. Discourse in publications and social media are full of alarmist discussions which fixate on the myriad points of divergence and warn of an inevitable clash of these civilizations. Absent are any meaningful proposals that address potential points of convergence.

Building mutual trust through cooperative medical care holds true potential. Healthcare surpasses borders. The universal feeling of compassion for one in need allows medical workers from any cultural background to cooperate. Helping another in need is a basic human motivation.

What can we as individuals do? We started with two words *Love Key* that sounded like our name Loeffke. Then a talented artist, Carmen Queral, drew a warrior on a horse. His right hand is holding ten wellness lessons. His left hand a shield with a heart and a key. We use this image as our calling card. The message is simple. Love is the key to friendship. Caring for others will even conquer hate. We need a continuous dialogue. Many have yet to learn:

"When we stop talking people start dying." Many of us are the wounded and the dead because of a policy that for 18 years did not allow shaking hands with Chinese diplomats.

I am one of those wounded. My West Point classmate was killed by a Chinese mine and Sgt. Larry Morford who helped save and change my life was killed by a Chinese bullet. All this could have been prevented if we had been talking.

Promoting peace is best realized by cooperating in actions that enhance the health of our world. We will go anywhere to teach wellness. It is our bridge to peace. We use a Wellness Magic Book that depending on how we hold it, the pages change colors and disappear. Visit www.helpingotherstoday.com and see the Wellness Magic Book in the short video.

We hope you will join us in making friends and the world healthier.

May your parachutes open and your landings soft